HEALING SCHOOL

HEALING SCHOOL
THE PERFECT PLAN FOR CONNECTING TO GOD'S PERFECT WILL CONCERNING HEALING

VOLUME 1

DR. KEVIN L. ZADAI

© Copyright 2024 Kevin L. Zadai. All rights reserved. This book is protected by the copyright laws of the United States of America. This book may not be copied or reprinted for commercial gain or profit. The use of short quotations or the copying of an occasional page for personal or group study is permitted and encouraged. Permission will be granted upon request. Unless otherwise indicated, Scripture quotations are taken from the New King James Version. Copyright © 1982 by Thomas Nelson, Inc. Used by permission. All rights reserved.

Scripture quotations marked (NLT) are taken from the Holy Bible, New Living Translation, copyright ©1996, 2004, 2015 by Tyndale House Foundation. Used by permission of Tyndale House Publishers, a Division of Tyndale House Ministries, Carol Stream, Illinois 60188. "Scripture quotations taken from the Amplified® Bible (AMPC), Copyright © 1954, 1958, 1962, 1964, 1965, 1987 by The Lockman Foundation. Used by permission. lockman.org." Scripture quotations marked (TPT) are from The Passion Translation®. Copyright © 2017, 2018 by Passion & Fire Ministries, Inc. Used by permission. All rights reserved. www.thePassionTranslation.com.

Please note that Warrior Notes publishing style capitalizes certain pronouns in Scripture that refer to the Father, Son, and Holy Spirit, which may differ from some publishers' styles. Take note that the name "satan" and related names are not capitalized. We choose not to acknowledge him, even to the point of violating accepted grammatical rules. The author and Warrior Notes have made an intentional decision to italicize many Scriptures in block quotes.

Warrior Notes Publishing
P O Box 1288
Destrehan, LA 70047

Cover design: Virtually Possible Designs

Reach us on the internet: www.Kevinzadai.com. For more information about our school, go to www.warriornotesschool.com.

ISBN 13 tp:978-1-6631-0103-7
ISBN 13 ebook: 978-1-6631-0104-4

DEDICATION

I dedicate this book to the Lord Jesus Christ. When I died during surgery and met with Jesus on the other side, He insisted that I return to life on the earth and that I help people with their destinies. Because of Jesus's love and concern for people, the Lord has actually chosen to send a person back from death to help everyone who will receive that help so that their destiny and purpose are secure in Him.

I want You, Lord, to know that when You come to take me to be with You someday, I sincerely hope that people don't remember me but remember the revelation of Jesus Christ that You have shown through me. I want others to know that I am merely being obedient to Your heavenly calling and mission, which is to reveal Your plan for the fulfillment of the divine destiny for each of God's children.

ACKNOWLEDGMENTS

In addition to sharing my story with everyone through the book *Heavenly Visitation: A Guide to the Supernatural,* God has commissioned me to write over sixty books and study guides. Most recently, the Lord gave me the commission to release this book, *Healing School Volume 1.* I want to thank everyone who has encouraged me, assisted me, and prayed for me during the writing of this work. Special thanks to my wonderful wife, Kathi, for her love and dedication to the Lord and me. Thank you to a great staff for the wonderful job editing this book.

CONTENTS

Introduction 1

Isaiah 53:1 3

Isaiah 53:2 5

Isaiah 53:3 7

Isaiah 53:4 9

Isaiah 53:5 11

Isaiah 53:6 13

Isaiah 53:7 15

Isaiah 53:8 17

Isaiah 53:9 19

Isaiah 53:10 21

Isaiah 53:11 23

Isaiah 53:12 25

INTRODUCTION

Welcome to Healing School! In this volume, we will examine Isaiah 53, which prophesies Jesus' coming and bearing of our sins and sicknesses. Keep this book with you for your personal study and connect with God's perfect will concerning healing.

God bless you!

Kevin Zadai

DR. KEVIN L. ZADAI

THE PERFECT PLAN FOR CONNECTING TO GOD'S PERFECT WILL CONCERNING HEALING

Who has believed our message? To whom has the LORD revealed his powerful arm?

—ISAIAH 53:1 NLT—

Isaiah 53:1 AMPC:
- Who has believed (trusted in, relied upon, and clung to)
- our message [of that which was revealed to us]?
- And to whom has the arm of the Lord been disclosed?

Isaiah 53:1 TPT:

Who has truly believed our revelation? To whom will Yahweh reveal his mighty arm?

Isaiah 53:1 NKJV:

Who has believed our report? And to whom has the arm of the LORD been revealed? For He shall grow up before Him as a tender plant,

NOTES:

THE PERFECT PLAN FOR CONNECTING TO GOD'S PERFECT WILL CONCERNING HEALING

My servant grew up in the LORD's presence like a tender green shoot, like a root in dry ground. There was nothing beautiful or majestic about his appearance, nothing to attract us to him.

—ISAIAH 53:2 NLT—

Isaiah 53:2 <u>AMPC</u>:
- For [the Servant of God] grew up before Him like a tender plant,
- and like a root out of dry ground;
- He has no form or comeliness [royal, kingly pomp],
- that we should look at Him,

- and no beauty that we should desire Him.

Isaiah 53:2 TPT:

He sprouted up like a tender plant before the Lord, like a root in parched soil. He possessed no distinguishing beauty or outward splendor to catch our attention—nothing special in his appearance to make us desire him.

Isaiah 53:2 NKJV:

For He shall grow up before Him as a tender plant, And as a root out of dry ground. He has no form or comeliness; And when we see Him, *There is* no beauty that we should desire Him.

NOTES:

_____
_____
_____
_____
_____
_____
_____
_____

THE PERFECT PLAN FOR CONNECTING TO GOD'S PERFECT WILL CONCERNING HEALING

He was despised and rejected—a man of sorrows, acquainted with deepest grief. We turned our backs on him and looked the other way. He was despised, and we did not care.

—ISAIAH 53:3 NLT—

Isaiah 53:3 AMPC:
- He was despised and rejected *and* forsaken by men,
- a Man of sorrows *and* pains,
- and acquainted with grief

- *and* sickness;
- and like One from Whom men hide their faces
- He was despised,
- and we did not appreciate His worth
- *or* have any esteem for Him.

Isaiah 53:3 TPT:

He was despised and rejected by men, a man of *deep* sorrows who was no stranger to suffering and grief. We hid our faces from him in disgust and considered him a nobody, not worthy of respect.

Isaiah 53:3 NKJV:

He is despised and rejected by men, A Man of sorrows and acquainted with grief. And we hid, as it were, *our* faces from Him; He was despised, and we did not esteem Him.

NOTES:

_____
_____
_____
_____
_____
_____

THE PERFECT PLAN FOR CONNECTING TO GOD'S PERFECT WILL CONCERNING HEALING

Yet it was our weaknesses he carried; it was our sorrows that weighed him down. And we thought his troubles were a punishment from God, a punishment for his own sins!

—ISAIAH 53:4 NLT—

Isaiah 53:4 <u>AMPC:</u>

- Surely He has borne our griefs (sicknesses, weaknesses, and distresses)
- and carried our sorrows
- *and* pains [of punishment],
- yet we [ignorantly] considered Him stricken,

- smitten,
- and afflicted by God [as if with leprosy].

Isaiah 53:4 TPT:

Yet he was the one who carried our sicknesses and endured the torment of our sufferings. We viewed him as one who was being punished for something he himself had done, as one who was struck down by God and brought low.

Isaiah 53:4 NKJV:

Surely He has borne our griefs And carried our sorrows; Yet we esteemed Him stricken, Smitten by God, and afflicted.

NOTES:

_____
_____
_____
_____
_____
_____
_____
_____
_____

THE PERFECT PLAN FOR CONNECTING TO GOD'S PERFECT WILL CONCERNING HEALING

But he was pierced for our rebellion, crushed for our sins. He was beaten so we could be whole. He was whipped so we could be healed.

ISAIAH 53:5 NLT—

Isaiah 53:5 AMPC:
- But He was wounded for our transgressions,
- He was bruised for our guilt
- *and* iniquities;
- the chastisement [needful to obtain] peace *and* well-being for us was upon Him,
- and with the stripes [that wounded] Him
- we are healed *and* made whole.

Isaiah 53:5 TPT:
But it was because of our rebellious deeds that he was pierced and because of our sins that he was crushed. He endured the punishment that made us completely whole, and in his wounding we found our healing.

Isaiah 53:5 NKJV:
But He *was* wounded for our transgressions, *He was* bruised for our iniquities; The chastisement for our peace *was* upon Him, And by His stripes we are healed.

NOTES:
_____
_____
_____
_____
_____
_____
_____
_____
_____
_____
_____
_____
_____
_____

THE PERFECT PLAN FOR CONNECTING TO GOD'S PERFECT WILL CONCERNING HEALING

*All of us, like sheep, have strayed away. We have left God's paths to follow our own. Yet the L*ORD *laid on him the sins of us all.*

—ISAIAH 53:6 NLT—

Isaiah 53:6 AMPC:
- All we like sheep have gone astray,
- we have turned everyone to his own way;
- and the Lord has made to light upon Him
- the guilt
- *and* iniquity of us all.

Isaiah 53:6 TPT:

Like wayward sheep, we have all wandered astray. Each of us has turned from God's paths and chosen our own way; even so, Yahweh laid the guilt of our every sin upon him.

Isaiah 53:6 <u>NKJV:</u>

All we like sheep have gone astray; We have turned, every one, to his own way; And the LORD [n]has laid on Him the iniquity of us all.

NOTES:

_____
_____
_____
_____
_____
_____
_____
_____
_____
_____
_____
_____
_____
_____

THE PERFECT PLAN FOR CONNECTING TO GOD'S PERFECT WILL CONCERNING HEALING

He was oppressed and treated harshly, yet he never said a word. He was led like a lamb to the slaughter. And as a sheep is silent before the shearers, he did not open his mouth.

—ISAIAH 53:7 NLT—

Isaiah 53:7 AMPC:
- He was oppressed,
- [yet when] He was afflicted,
- He was submissive
- *and* opened not His mouth;
- like a lamb that is led to the slaughter,

- and as a sheep before her shearers is dumb,
- so He opened not His mouth.

Isaiah 53:7 TPT:

He was oppressed and harshly mistreated; still he humbly submitted, refusing to defend himself. He was led like a *gentle* lamb to be slaughtered. Like a silent sheep before his shearers, he didn't even open his mouth.

Isaiah 53:7 NKJV:

He was oppressed and He was afflicted, Yet He opened not His mouth; He was led as a lamb to the slaughter, And as a sheep before its shearers is silent, So He opened not His mouth.

NOTES:

_____
_____
_____
_____
_____
_____
_____

THE PERFECT PLAN FOR CONNECTING TO GOD'S PERFECT WILL CONCERNING HEALING

Unjustly condemned, he was led away. No one cared that he died without descendants, that his life was cut short in midstream. But he was struck down for the rebellion of my people.

—ISAIAH 53:8 NLT—

Isaiah 53:8 <u>AMPC:</u>
- By oppression and judgment He was taken away;
- and as for His generation,
- who among them considered that He was cut off out of the land of the living

- [stricken to His death] for the transgression of my [Isaiah's] people,
- to whom the stroke was due?

Isaiah 53:8 TPT:
By coercion and with a perversion of justice he was taken away. And who could have imagined his future? He was cut down in the prime of life; for the rebellion of his own people, he was struck down *in their* place.

Isaiah 53:8 NKJV:
He was taken from prison and from judgment, And who will declare His generation? For He was cut off from the land of the living; For the transgressions of My people He was stricken.

NOTES:
_____
_____
_____
_____
_____
_____
_____

THE PERFECT PLAN FOR CONNECTING TO GOD'S PERFECT WILL CONCERNING HEALING

He had done no wrong and had never deceived anyone. But he was buried like a criminal; he was put in a rich man's grave.

—ISAIAH 53:9 NLT—

Isaiah 53:9 <u>AMPC:</u>
- And they assigned Him a grave with the wicked,
- and with a rich man in His death,
- although He had done no violence,
- neither was any deceit in His mouth.

Isaiah 53:9 <u>TPT</u>:
They gave him a grave among criminals, but he ended up instead in a rich man's tomb, although he had done no violence nor spoken deceitfully.

Isaiah 53:9 <u>NKJV</u>:
And they made His grave with the wicked—But with the rich at His death, Because He had done no violence, Nor *was any* deceit in His mouth.

NOTES:

THE PERFECT PLAN FOR CONNECTING TO GOD'S PERFECT WILL CONCERNING HEALING

But it was the LORD's good plan to crush him and cause him grief. Yet when his life is made an offering for sin, he will have many descendants. He will enjoy a long life, and the LORD's good plan will prosper in his hands.

—ISAIAH 53:10 NLT—

Isaiah 53:10 AMPC:
- Yet it was the will of the Lord to bruise Him;
- He has put Him to grief *and* made Him sick.
- When You *and* He make His life an offering for sin

- [and He has risen from the dead, in time to come],
- He shall see His [spiritual] offspring,
- He shall prolong His days,
- and the will *and* pleasure of the Lord shall prosper in His hand.

Isaiah 53:10 TPT:
Even though it pleased Yahweh to crush him with grief, he will be restored to favor. After his soul becomes a guilt-offering, he will gaze upon his many offspring and prolong his days. And through him, Yahweh's deepest desires will be fully accomplished.

Isaiah 53:10 NKJV:
Yet it pleased the LORD to bruise Him; He has put *Him* to grief. When You make His soul an offering for sin, He shall see *His* seed, He shall prolong *His* days, And the pleasure of the LORD shall prosper in His hand.

NOTES:

_____
_____
_____
_____
_____
_____

THE PERFECT PLAN FOR CONNECTING TO GOD'S PERFECT WILL CONCERNING HEALING

When he sees all that is accomplished by his anguish, he will be satisfied. And because of his experience, my righteous servant will make it possible for many to be counted righteous, for he will bear all their sins.

—ISAIAH 53:11 NLT—

Isaiah 53:11 AMPC:
- He shall see [the fruit] of the travail of His soul and be satisfied;
- by His knowledge of Himself [which He possesses and imparts to others]
- shall My [uncompromisingly] righteous One,
- My Servant,

- justify many *and* make many righteous (upright and in right standing with God), for He shall bear their iniquities *and* their guilt [with the consequences, says the Lord].

Isaiah 53:11 TPT:

After the great anguish of his soul, he will see light and be fully satisfied. By knowing him, the righteous one, my servant will make many to be righteous, because he, *their sin-bearer*, carried away their sins.

Isaiah 53:11 NKJV:

He shall see the labor of His soul, *and* be satisfied. By His knowledge My righteous Servant shall justify many, For He shall bear their iniquities.

NOTES:

_____
_____
_____
_____
_____
_____
_____
_____
_____

THE PERFECT PLAN FOR CONNECTING TO GOD'S PERFECT WILL CONCERNING HEALING

I will give him the honors of a victorious soldier, because he exposed himself to death. He was counted among the rebels. He bore the sins of many and interceded for rebels.

—ISAIAH 53:12 NLT—

Isaiah 53:12 AMPC:
- Therefore will I divide Him a portion with the great [kings and rulers],
- and He shall divide the spoil with the mighty,
- because He poured out His life unto death,
- and [He let Himself] be regarded as a criminal

- *and* be numbered with the transgressors;
- yet He bore [and took away] the sin of many
- and made intercession for the transgressors (the rebellious).

Isaiah 53:12 <u>NLT</u>:

So I, *Yahweh*, will assign him a portion among a great multitude, *and he will triumph* and divide the spoils of victory with *his* mighty ones —all because he poured out his life-blood to death. He was counted among the worst of sinners, yet he carried sin's burden for many and interceded for those who were rebels.

Isaiah 53:12 <u>NKJV</u>:

Therefore I will divide Him a portion with the great, And He shall divide the spoil with the strong, Because He poured out His soul unto death, And He was numbered with the transgressors, And He bore the sin of many, And made intercession for the transgressors.

NOTES:

_____
_____
_____
_____
_____

HEALING SCHOOL: VOLUME ONE

ADDITIONAL NOTES:

HEALING SCHOOL: VOLUME ONE

SALVATION PRAYER

Lord God,
I confess that I am a sinner.
I confess that I need Your Son, Jesus.
Please forgive me in His name.
Lord Jesus, I believe You died for me and that
You are alive and listening to me now.
I now turn from my sins and welcome You into my heart. Come
and take control of my life.
Make me the kind of person You want me to be.
Now, fill me with Your Holy Spirit, who will show me how to live
for You. I acknowledge You before men as my Savior and my
Lord. In Jesus's name. Amen.

If you prayed this prayer, please contact us at
info@kevinzadai.com
for more information and materials.

We welcome you to join our network at Warriornotes.tv for access to exclusive programming.

To enroll in our ministry school, go to:
www.Warriornotesschool.com.

Visit www.KevinZadai.com
for additional ministry materials.

ABOUT DR. KEVIN ZADAI

Kevin Zadai, Th.D., was called to the ministry at the age of ten. He attended Central Bible College in Springfield, Missouri, where he received a Bachelor of Arts in theology. Later, he received training in missions at Rhema Bible College and a Th. D. at Primus University. Dr. Kevin L. Zadai is dedicated to training Christians to live and operate in two realms at once— the supernatural and the natural. At age 31, Kevin met Jesus, got a second chance at life, and received a revelation that he could not fail because it's all rigged in our favor! Kevin holds a commercial pilot license and is retired from Southwest Airlines after twenty-nine years as a flight attendant. Kevin is the founder and president of Warrior Notes School of Ministry. He and his lovely wife, Kathi, reside in New Orleans, Louisiana.

WARRIOR NOTES
SCHOOL OF MINISTRY

ENROLL IN DAYS OF HEAVEN ON EARTH AND HEAVENLY VISITATION AT NO COST!

FREE ENROLLMENT

WARRIORNOTESSCHOOL.COM

EARN YOUR ASSOCIATE, BACHELOR, MASTER, OR DOCTORATE DEGREES WITH DR. KEVIN ZADAI!

Master's
Doctorate

Associate's
Bachelor's

WARRIOR NOTES SCHOOL OF MINISTRY IS AN ACCREDITED BIBLE COLLEGE

CHECK OUT other materials on Healing
by Dr. Kevin L. Zadai

*Kevin has written over sixty books and study guides.
Please see our website for a complete list of materials!
Kevinzadai.com*